FLUTE REPERTOIRE

TELEMANN
12 Fantasias for Flute Solo, TWV 40:2–13

Urtext

Revised by Masahiro ARITA

テレマン
無伴奏フルートのための
12のファンタジー　TWV 40:2–13

［原典版］

有田正広 校訂

音楽之友社

はじめに Introduction	2
12のファンタジー（現代譜） 12 Fantasias (Modern notation)	6
12のファンタジー（初版譜ファクシミリ） 12 Fantasias (Facsimile of the first edition)	30
校訂報告 Textual notes	43
各曲のスタイル Stylistic feautures of each piece	44
用語小辞典　〜18世紀音楽を演奏するために Glossary of musical terms: for performance of 18th century music	45
参考文献 Bibliography	48

ONGAKU NO TOMO EDITION

はじめに

有田正広

無伴奏音楽

　単音楽器、あるいは旋律楽器（フルートやヴァイオリン、チェロなど）のための無伴奏作品に、作曲家は何を託すのだろう？ 単旋律、またはそれに準じた書法で書かれた楽譜の背景には、そこに敢えて書き表されなかった音の存在が想像され、その先には深く広い音楽の世界が広がっている。

　作曲家にとってこの分野の音楽を作ることは、いわば創意と霊感への大いなる試み、挑戦に他ならない。

　バロック時代に残された無伴奏作品を俯瞰[*1]すると、そこには選ばれた楽器の奏法を追求し、極限の表現方法の可能性を開拓する意思と、それを可能にした演奏家の存在を想像することができる。

　無伴奏作品を演奏する上でもっとも重要なことは、楽譜には記されていなくても音の背後に確実に存在している、他の声部やハーモニーに耳を傾け、無音と有音の間を行き来し、更には沈黙などの繊細なニュアンスの世界を表現することだろう。

テレマンのファンタジー

　テレマン（1681〜1767）が残した「ファンタジー」と題される作品は、フルート、ヴァイオリン、ヴィオラ・ダ・ガンバの各12曲ずつ。またチェンバロとオルガンのための作品[*2]を合わせると少なくとも73曲に及ぶ。

　ファンタジー [Fantasy, Fantasie, Fantasia *etc.*] という用語は時代の流れの中で、その意味を少しずつ変化させていった。「ファンタジー」の語は、今日の「形式にとらわれない自由な作曲」という意味とは異なり、この語が用いられはじめた16世紀中頃には、作曲家が神の啓示として与えられた霊感を基に、内在する音楽の閃き（＝ファンタジー）を自由に喚起させながらも、厳格な数比を用いた対位法による作品や即興演奏のことを指していた。その後17世紀からのいわゆる「バロック時代」のファンタジーには次第に人間の持つ感情や美学的な表現などの要素が取り入れられるようになるが、未だそれ以前の数比的＝対位法的な様式を色濃く残してもいた。18世紀中頃になると、17世紀の様式、形式の基本的要素を保ちながらも感情表現や音響的な表現方法を用いることで徐々に「自由性」が表出されるようになる。たとえばJ. S. バッハのBWV 903、904、906、917、918、919、922、944、C. Ph. E. バッハのWq. 58-6、58-7、59-5、59-6、61-3、61-6、67、80、117-8〜16、そしてモーツァルトのKV 396、397、457、624、Anh. 32 などが「ファンタジー」の系譜と変遷を物語っている。

Introduction

Masahiro Arita

Music without accompaniment

What are a composer's intentions when writing monophonic music or works for unaccompanied melodic instruments such as the flute, the violin and the cello? Such music is underpinned by its appeal to the imagination to flesh out the music and provide it with the notes not actually written in the musical notation, thus opening up onto a rich and expansive musical world.

For any composer, creating music of this type represents a major challenge to his creativity and inspiration. A glance at the whole range of works for unaccompanied instruments from the Baroque era reveals how composers strove to explore the technical and expressive possibilities of their chosen instruments, dependent as they were on the existence of performers capable of realising these possibilities.

The most important consideration when performing unaccompanied works is to listen to the other parts and harmonies that underpin the music but that do not actually appear in the musical notation, to move back and forth in the gap between sound and absence of sound, and to express a world of subtle nuance as represented, for example, by silence.

The Fantasies of Telemann

Georg Philipp Telemann (1681–1767) composed twelve works with the title 'Fantasie' for each of three instruments, flute, violin and viola da gamba. The number of works with this title increases from 36 to 73 if the Fantasies for organ and harpsichord are also taken into account.

The meaning of the term 'Fantasie' (or its variants such as Fantasy or Fantasia) in its varied forms differs slightly from one era to the next. Today we think of it as referring to a work with a free and uninhibited formal structure, but around the middle of the 16th century when the term first came into use it referred to works or improvisations rooted in strict contrapuntal principles based on inspiration received by the composer as a divine gift while at the same time giving full rein to the inherent musical fantasy implied by the name of the genre. Thereafter, with the advent of the Baroque era early in the 17th century, the 'Fantasie' gradually began to incorporate elements such as human emotions and aesthetic expression, while at the same time never losing the previously predominant sense of mathematical proportion and contrapuntal style. Around the middle of the 18th century a greater sense of freedom gradually began to predominate through the use of emotional and acoustic expressive means while preserving the basic stylistic and formal features characteristic of the 17th-century Fantasie. For instance, the lineage and changes in the concept of the Fantasie can be traced from works such as J.S. Bach's BWV 903, 904, 906, 917, 918, 919, 922 and 944 through C.P.E. Bach's Wq. 58-6, 58-7, 59-5, 61-3,

そして19世紀に入ると作曲者個人の感性を、形式から開放された自由な形式に反映させる音楽へと変化し、さらに19世紀後半には有名なオペラのアリアや人気の高い音楽を題材とする「主題と変奏」や「序奏」と「ファンタジー」を組み合わせた作品群がサロンで人気を得た。

日本では「ファンタジー」の訳語として「幻想曲」が用いられることが多いが、これは19世紀以降の、形式にとらわれない新しい「ファンタジー」に向けられた意味で用いられている。

テレマンの「ファンタジー」は、こうした歴史の流れの中で、17世紀以来の対位法的な要素を組み入れ、様々な様式と形式、たとえば舞曲やソナタの形式を彷彿とさせる書法を用い、作曲者の新しく自由な試みを加えた創意に富んだ音楽作品となっている。

無伴奏フルートのための12のファンタジー

この作品はテレマン自身の手による初版楽譜 "Fantasie per il Violino, senza Basso" を唯一の出典としている。タイトルページの右下方に鉛筆で "Telemann" と記され、この書体がテレマンの他の印刷譜の書体や自筆のサインと同じであることと、また楽譜の中にテレマン自身によるものと思われる幾つかの訂正が見られることから、この楽譜はテレマン自身が所有していたものと考えられる。

また、タイトルページに印刷された「ヴァイオリンのための」の表記にもかかわらず本作をフルートのための作品と判断する理由は、

1. 音域が18世紀のフルートの一般的な音域に限定されていること
2. 18世紀のヴァイオリン作品の一般的な音域のうち、フルートには演奏できない低音域や重音が全く使われていないこと（これは前述の『無伴奏ヴァイオリンのための12のファンタジー TWV 40:14-25』との比較からも明らかである）
3. 12曲の調の選択がこの時代のフルートを想定していること

などにある。

テレマンはここでフルートという単音の旋律楽器によって、旋律の持つ美しさや表情の可能性だけではなく、p. 44の《各曲のスタイル》でも触れているように、幅広い跳躍や分散和音などのパッセージを用いた対位法的書法や和声の表現を成し遂げている。そしてイタリア語による速度記号、表情記号のみが記される全12曲の中の様々な「部分」——「楽章」という概念を持たない記譜法を用いていることから敢えて「部分」と呼ぶ——には一つとして同じ形式の曲はなく、全12曲は18世紀の器楽作品における様々な様式感と多様性とを持ちあわせた作品となっている。

61-6, 67, 80, 117-8 to 16, to Mozart's KV396, 397, 457, 624 and Anh. 32.

As the 19th century got under way, the Fantasie turned into a genre in which the personal feelings of the composer were reflected in free form liberated from all formal restraints. In the latter half of the 19th century, works combining themes and variations based on famous opera arias and popular music along with overtures and Fantasies became popular in musical salons.

Within this historical process, Telemann's Fantasies incorporate contrapuntal elements characteristic of the genre from the 17th century onwards in a style that evokes a variety of forms and styles such as dance pieces and sonata form, while at the same time evincing the composer's rich invention and attempts to break out in a new and freer direction.

Twelve Fantasies for Unaccompanied Flute

The sole source for this set of works is the first edition of the *Fantasie per il Violino, senza Basso* in Telemann's own hand. The composer's name appears in pencil at the bottom right of the title page in a form identical to that employed on other printed scores and to his personal signature. The notation also includes several corrections that would appear to have been made by Telemann himself, suggesting that it was owned by him.

The reasons for assuming that these works were intended for performance on the flute despite the specification 'per il Violino' printed on the title page are as follows:

1. The pitch range is restricted to the standard range of the 18th–century flute.
2. The fact that no use is made of the bottom fifth of the standard range of the 18th–century violin, which lies outside the range of the flute, or of double stopping. This feature sets these works apart from the previously mentioned *Twelve Fantasies for Violin Solo*, TWV 40–14 to 25, which do make use of the violin's full pitch range.
3. The selection of the keys of these twelve pieces is clearly premised upon the flute used during the era when the works were composed.

As mentioned on page 44 in the section on Style, Telemann's intention in these pieces was not merely to pursue melodic beauty and the expressive possibilities of the use of the flute as a monophonic melody instrument, but also to explore contrapuntal writing and harmony in passages featuring wide leaps and broken chords. The various sections of the twelve pieces (one hesitates to refer to them as 'movements' because of the nature of the musical notation) are marked solely with Italian tempo indications and expressive markings. None of these sections evince the same form and all twelve pieces possess the varied sense of style and the diversity that characterises instrumental works of the 18th century.

初版譜

初版譜に出版年が明記されていないことから、明確な出版年は特定できない。マッテゾン（1681〜1764）が1740年に著した『栄誉への基礎』にテレマンが寄稿した自伝に含まれる作品表には、本作が「1731〜33年の間に記された」とあることに加え、ヴァイオリンやヴィオラ・ダ・ガンバのためのファンタジーの出版年などから本作の初版は1732〜33年と考えられるが、近年では1731年かそれ以前の刊行とする学説も見られる。

現在、この初版譜はブリュッセル王立音楽院附属図書館所蔵、蔵書番号は littera T5823W / B-Bc 5823。

18世紀の記譜法

当版はテレマンが刻版した初版譜をもとに、可能な限り作者の意図を正確に伝えるように作成した。テレマンが生きた18世紀中頃までの記譜法 Notation には現代の習慣とは異なる点がいくつかある。

1. 臨時記号

現代では臨時記号は付けられた音符以降その小節全体について有効だが、おおよそ18世紀中頃までは、臨時記号は基本的には付けられた音符のみに有効で、本位記号（♮）が無い場合でも元の音に戻される（ファンタジー第12番第22、33小節など）。しかしテレマン時代の記譜法を現代の楽譜に持ち込むと混乱を来すため、本版では現代の記譜法に従って臨時記号を記した。

2. 連桁

テレマンは複数の箇所で、現代の記譜法とは異なった方法で連桁を用いて音楽表現上の意図を明確にしている（たとえば第1番第12〜13小節 ♫♫♫♫｜♫♫♫♫ や第8番第42小節 ♩♪ ♪♫♫♫ など）。これは内在する和声などから導き出されるべき拍感や表情を明確にし、あるいは同じ和声進行や反復進行（ゼクエンツ）における様々な表現変化を視覚的に受け止めやすくするための、演奏者に向けた指針となっている。こうした、連桁による記譜表現の例は、テレマン以外にもたとえばマラン・マレ、コレッリ、ヴィヴァルディ、J. S. バッハなどの作品中に見られるが、現代譜には生かされているものが少ないため、ファクシミリ譜を参考にすることを提案したい。

3. ＋（トリラー）

後には tr と書かれるようになったが、当時は＋記号で示すことが多かった。

4. Ⅰ（ストローク Stroke、ダガー Dagger、シュトリッヒ Strich、カイル Keil）

その音を強調する。後にはスタッカートあるいはアクセント記号へと分化していった。ストロークの表現には様々な可能性が

First edition

The date of publication does not appear in the first edition and it is not possible to specify the actual year. In the list of works included in the autobiography that Telemann submitted to the *Grundlage einer Ehren–Pforte* (Foundation of a Portal of Honour, 1740) compiled by Johann Mattheson (1681–1764), the work is given the dating 1731 to 1733. Considering the dates of publication of the Fantasies for violin and viola da gamba, a dating of 1732 or 1733 would seem appropriate, although in recent years some scholars have posited a date of publication of 1731 or earlier.

The original edition of the work is in the possession of the library 'Conservatoire royal – Koninklijk Conservatorium', Brussels. (catalogue number littera T5823W / B-Bc 5823).

Musical notation in the 18th century

This edition has been prepared on the basis of the original edition engraved by Telemann in such a way as to convey the composer's intentions as accurately as possible. There are several differences between the notation employed until around the middle of the 18th century when Telemann was active and the notation in general use today.

1. Accidentals

Accidentals when used today apply throughout the bar after their first appearance in a bar. However, in Telemann's time an accidental generally applied solely to the note to which it was attached, and a natural sign (♮) did not have to be attached to a note in order to cancel out the previous sharp or flat. (See, for example, bars 22 and 33 in Fantasia XII.) In order to avoid the confusion likely to result from incorporating Telemann's notational practice into modern notation, I have therefore followed modern conventions with regard to accidentals in this edition.

2. Beams

In various places Telemann uses beams in a manner different from modern notational practice with the aim of clarifying his intentions as regards musical expression. (See, for example, bars 12 and 13 of Fantasia 1. ♫♫♫♫｜♫♫♫♫ and bar 42 of Fantasia 8. ♩♪ ♪♫♫♫. The composer's intention here is to provide guidance to the performer by clarifying the metrical and expressive properties of the music inherent in the latent harmonic structure and to provide a visual representation of varied expressive nature of the same harmonic progressions and sequences. Similar examples of the use of notation for expressive purposes are to be also in works by Marain Marais, Corelli, Vivaldi and J.S. Bach, but few are still employed in modern notation. I would suggest therefore that the facsimile notation be referred to in this regard.

3. ＋: Trills

Trills in Telemann's time were written using the sign ＋, and it was

潜んでいて、「強調」は一概にプラス方向（*sf*／*rf*／*f*／*fz*など の強い表現）とは限らず、時には「弱音」や、出音のタイミング と表現のコントロール（サスペンション、ポルタメントなど）に よって演奏される場合もあるので要注意。

5. 強弱
「*f*」「*p*」「何も書かない」の3段階によって示すことが一般的 だったが、実際の強弱が3段階だったわけではない。*pp*から*ff* まで、あるいはそれ以上の階調での表現が演奏者には委ねられ ている。

only at a later date that the *tr* sign came into general use.

4. |: Strokes, daggers
These symbols were used to represent accents and later separated into staccato and accent signs. There are various latent possibilities concerning interpretation of strokes. Care is needed since the idea of placing emphasis on a particular note does not necessarily imply a strong accent in the form of *sf*, *rf*, *f* or *fz*, and may sometimes indicate a quiet sound, the timing of a particular note or expressive control in forms such as suspensions and portamentos.

5. Dynamics
The standard convention is to use the indications *f* or *p* or to give no dynamic marking at all, but this should not be taken to mean that there are actually three different dynamic levels. Use of dynamics from pianissimo to fortissimo and beyond is otherwise left to the discretion of the performer.

TWV 番号

テレマンの作品群に付けられた作品番号。ルーンケが編纂し 1984年にベーレンライター社から「G. Ph. テレマン：主題的―体 系的作品目録／テレマン作品目録 Georg Philipp Telemann Thematisch-Systematisches Verzeichnis seiner Werke / Telemann Werkverzeichnis (TWV)」のタイトルで出版された。

ルーンケは様々な作品をカテゴライズし、通奏低音を伴わな い室内楽作品はTWV 40:に分類した。TWV 40:1として通奏低音 を伴わない、ヴィオラ・ダ・ガンバのためのソナタ ニ長調（『忠 実な音楽の師』ハンブルク、自費出版1728年）があることから、 『無伴奏フルートのための12のファンタジー』にはTWV 40:2か ら13までが付番されている。

TWV numbers

The works of Telemann are numbered in their printed editions in accordance with the *Telemann Werkverzeichnis* (TWV, or in full the *Georg Philipp Telemann Thematisch-Systematisches Verzeichnis seiner Werke*) compiled by the Telemann scholar Martin Ruhnke and published by Bärenreiter in 1984.

On the basis of a classification of Telemann's oeuvre, Ruhnke gave the chamber works for solo instruments without basso continuo the catalogue number TWV 40. TWV 40:1 is the number of the Sonata in D major for viola da gamba without basso continuo that forms part of the collection known as *Der Getreuer Music-Meister* (Hamburg, 1728), whereas the Twelve Fantasias for Flute without basso continuo bear the numbers TWV 40:2 to 40:13.

(Translation: Robin Thompson)

---

*1　17〜18世紀に見られる代表的な無伴奏作品 / Representative unaccompanied works from the 17th and 18th centuries for melody instruments

Published/Composed year	Instrument	Composer	Title
1675	Violin	Biber, Heinrich Ignaz Franz von	Passacaglia (from "*Rosenkranz Sonaten*"),
1696	Violin	Westhoff, Johann Paul von	6 Part ita à Violino senza Basso accompagnato
1708/1715	Flute	Hotteterre, Jacques	Eco, pour la Flûte traversiere sans Basse continue
1720	Violin	Bach, Johann Sebastian	Sei Solo a Violino senza Basso accompagnato, BWV 1001–6
*ca.*1720	Violoncello	Bach, Johann Sebastian	6 Suites a Violoncello Solo senza Basso, BWV 1007–12
ca. 1720	Violin	Pisendel, Johann Georg	Sonata il Violino solo senza Basso, a-moll
*ca.*1725	Flute	Bach, Johann Sebastian	Solo (Part ita), a-moll, BWV 1013
1728	Viola da gamba	Telemann, Georg Philipp	Sonata D-dur, für Viola da Gamba, from "*Der getreue Music-Meister*", TWV 40:1
ca. 1731	Flute	Telemann, Georg Philipp	(12) Fantasie per il Violino *(sic!)*, senza Basso, TWV 40:2–13
1735	Violin	Telemann, Goerg Philipp	XII Fantasie per il Violino, senza Basso, TWV 40: 14–25
1735–36	Viola da Gamba	Telemann, Georg Philipp	(12) Fantasies pour la Basse de Violle, TWV 40: 26–37
1744	Flute	Blavet, Michel	Gigue en Rondeau/ Rondeau, "1*er* Recuel de pieces"
1747/63	Flute	Bach, Carl Philipp Emmanuel	Sonata … Flauto Traverso Solo Senza Basso, a-moll, Wq. 132
ca. 1780	Bass Viol	Abel, Carl Friedrich	27 Pieces for Bass viol, WK 186212

*2　テレマン作曲のファンタジー　Fantasies of Telemann

Published/Composed Year	Instrument	Title
1728	Viola da gamba	Sonata D-dur, für Viola da Gamba, from "*Der getreue Music-Meister*", TWV 40:1
ca. 1731	Flute	(12) Fantasie per il Violino *(sic!)*, senza Basso, TWV 40:2–13
1732–33	Harpsichord	Fantasies pour Le Clavessin: 3 Douzaines, TWV33:1–36
1735	Violin	XII Fantasie per il Violino, senza Basso, TWV 40:14–25
1735–36	Viola da gamba	(12) Fantasies pour la Basse de Violle, TWV 40:26–37
ca. 1790	Organ	Fantasie für Orgel, D-Dur, TWV Anh. 33:3 (doubtful work. copied by other hand in 1790)

12 FANTASIAS

FANTASIA 1.

A dur / A major / La majeur / La maggiore / イ長調

Georg Philipp Telemann, TWV 40:2

FANTASIA 2.

a moll / a minor / la mineur / la minore / イ短調

TWV 40:3

FANTASIA 3.

h moll / b minor / si mineur / si minore / ロ短調

TWV 40:4

FANTASIA 4.

B dur / B flat major / Si bémol majeur / Si bemolle maggiore / 変ロ長調

TWV 40:5

FANTASIA 5.

C dur / C major / Ut majeur / Do maggiore / ハ長調

TWV 40:6

*1 初版譜ファクシミリの記譜に準じた。小節途中に次の拍子記号 ₵ がアウフタクトで置かれ、拍数が足りない不完全小節だが、作曲者が敢えて休符を置かなかったと判断した / In accordance with the facsimile of the first edition. The next time signature ₵ is placed on the upbeat in the middle of the bar. This is an imperfect bar with insufficient beats, but it would appear that the composer deliberately did not insert a rest at this point

FANTASIA 6.

d moll / d minor / re mineur / re minore / 二短調

TWV 40:7

FANTASIA 7.

D dur / D major / Re majeur / Re maggiore / 二長調

TWV 40:8

*1 「フランス風に」の意。p. 45の French overture の項を参照。
 "In the French style". For further information see 'French overture' in the Glossary (p. 46).

FANTASIA 8.

e moll / e minor / mi mineur / mi minore / ホ短調

TWV 40:9

FANTASIA 9.

E dur / E major / Mi majeur / Mi maggiore / ホ長調

TWV 40:10

FANTASIA X.

fis moll / f sharp minor / fa dièse mineur / fa diesis minore / 嬰ヘ短調

TWV 40:11

FANTASIA XI.

G dur / G major / Sol majeur / Sol maggiore / ト長調

TWV 40:12

*3 seems to be a valid performance possibility

FANTASIA XII.

g moll / g minor / sol mineur / sol minore / ト短調

TWV 40:13

初版譜ファクシミリ　A facsimile of the first edition

Printed with the kind permission of Library 'Conservatoire royal – Koninklijk Conservatorium' Brussels.

初版譜では見開きの左ページに空白、右ページに楽譜が一曲ずつ置かれている。本版では空白ページを除いたタイトルページおよび楽譜ページのみを掲載した。

In the first edition the left of two facing pages is empty and a single piece is set in each case on the right page. In this edition we have included the title page without the empty page and the pages with notation only.

littera T5823W / B-Bc 5823

page 1
(title)

校訂報告

以下の報告中、n:mは第n小節第m音を示す（TWV番号を除く）。
たとえば23:9は23小節目の第9音。

Fantasia 1, A major, TWV 40:2
- *1 23:9 作曲者によって ♪ から ♪ に訂正。
- *2 31:1 ƒ の欠落を補足。
- *3 32:1 初版譜のƒの位置を第3音から第1音に訂正。

Fantasia 2, a minor, TWV 40:3
- *1 8:4 作曲者によって ♪ から ♪ に訂正。
- *2 51:4 作曲者によって ♪ から ♪ に訂正。
- *3 64:4–8 初版譜でのリズム表記は ♪♪♪♪ 。本版ではこの後に続くリズムと同じ ♪♪♪♪ に訂正。
- *4 64:10, 12 初版譜は ♪ に見えるが不明瞭。本版では和声や旋律の理論から判断し、♪ とした。

Fantasia 4, B flat major, TWV 40:5
- *1 12:15 作曲者によって ♪ から ♪ に訂正。
- *2 86:4 初版譜では8分音符だが4分音符に訂正。

Fantasia 5, C major, TWV 40:6
- *1 8: 初版譜ファクシミリの記譜に準じた。小節途中に次の拍子記号Cがアウフタクトで置かれ、拍数が足りない不完全小節だが、作曲者が敢えて休符を置かなかったと判断した。
- *2 77:1, 4 ♪♪♪ とする版もあるが、初版譜に準じて ♪♪♪ とした。第75～77小節は第25～27小節に対応するものだが、作曲者が敢えて最後の終止形でバスの音に変化をつけた可能性があると校訂者は考える。
- *3 104:1–2 初版譜にはスラーがないが、第104小節に対応する第82、96小節では冒頭2音にスラーが付されていることから（　）付きのスラーを示した。しかし第82、96小節とは異なり第104小節は五度跳躍である。18世紀の演奏習慣から考えるとスラーを付けずに切り離して演奏することが一般的であり、作曲者が意図してスラーを記さなかった可能性が高い。

Fantasia 6, d minor, TWV 40:7
- *1 49:4 初版譜は ♪ の重音になっている。作曲者が ♪ を削除し忘れた可能性があると判断し ♪ を残した（第52小節を参照）。
- *2 85:1 初版譜では4分音符。作曲者によって2分音符に訂正。
- *3 96:4 作曲者によって ♪ を ♪ に訂正。

Fantasia 7, D major, TWV 40:8
- *1 1: 「フランス風に」の意。p. 45 のFrench overtureの項を参照。
- *2 7:1–2 & 8:1–2 初版譜のリズムは ♪♪♪♪ だが ♪♪♪♪ のリズムで演奏する。p. 45 のFrench overture の項を参照。
- *3 78:6 作曲者によって ♪ を ♪ に訂正。

Fantasia 8, e minor, TWV 40:9
- *1 14:5 初版譜にはfが記されているが、本版では作曲者の誤りと判断し削除した。
- *2 52:7 作曲者によって ♪ を ♪ に訂正。
- *3 61:2 初版譜がやや不明瞭で ♪ にも見える。これを採用している出版譜もあるが、本版ではこの箇所の和声（＝ ♪ の減七和音）を重視し ♪ を採用した。

Fantasia 9, E major, TWV 40:10
- *1 9: 初版譜には3拍目が無い。5小節目を参照し、休符が欠落していると判断した。
- *2 47:6 作曲者によって ♪ から ♪ に訂正。

Fantasia XI, G major, TWV 40:12
- *1 2:16 作曲者によって ♪ から ♪ に訂正。
- *2 7:14 作曲者によって ♪ から ♪ に訂正。
- *3 28: スペースの関係から初版譜では2拍分が欠落している。様々な可能性が考えられるが、4拍分に補う場合 ♪♪♪ のような演奏も考えられる。
- *4 42:4 初版譜が不明瞭なため、♪ か ♪ か判断が分かれる。この箇所の1拍目（属和音）から2拍目（主和音）への和声連結は第31、35、48、56小節と同様のパターンとみなせることから、本版ではこれらの小節と拍感の共通性がより高まる ♪ を採用した。第41小節第6音からの、下行する三度音程の下声部に含まれる順次進行を優先する場合は ♪ の採用も考えられる。

Fantasia XII, g minor, TWV 40:13
- *1 1:1 作曲者によって4分音符から2分音符に訂正。
- *2 67:5 作曲者によって ♪ から ♪ に訂正。

Textual notes

Numbers linked by a colon refer to the bar number followed by the position of the note within the bar, i.e. 23:9 means the 9th note of bar 23.

Fantasia 1, A major, TWV 40:2
- *1 23:9 Revised by the composer from ♪ to ♪.
- *2 31:1 Missing ƒ added.
- *3 32:1 Position of ƒ in the first edition revised from the third to the first note.

Fantasia 2, a minor, TWV 40:3
- *1 8:4 Revised by the composer from ♪ to ♪.
- *2 51:4 Revised by the composer from ♪ to ♪.
- *3 64:4–8 The rhythm in the first edition is ♪♪♪♪. Revised in the present edition to conform to the subsequent rhythm ♪♪♪♪.
- *4 64:10, 12 Appears in the first edition as ♪ but is unclear. Notated in the form of ♪ in this edition in accordance with harmonic and melodic theory.

Fantasia 4, B flat major, TWV 40:5
- *1 12:15 Revised by the composer from ♪ to ♪.
- *2 86:4 A quaver in the first edition but revised to a crotchet.

Fantasia 5, C major, TWV 40:6
- *1 8: In accordance with the facsimile of the first edition. The next time signature ₵ is placed on the upbeat in the middle of the bar. This is an imperfect bar with insufficient beats, but it would appear that the composer deliberately did not insert a rest at this point.
- *2 77:1, 4 Some editions give ♪♪♪, but I have followed the first edition, which gives ♪♪♪. Bars 75 to 77 correspond to bars 25 to 27, but I have revised this on the assumption that the composer may have employed the final cadence to vary the bass note.
- *3 104:1–2 There is no slur in the first edition, but the first two notes in bars 82 and 96, which correspond to bar 104, are slurred, on account of which I have added a slur in brackets. However, in contrast to bars 82 and 96, there is a leap of a fifth in bars 104. Eighteenth-century performance practice suggests that this passage would have been performed in a detached manner without attaching a slur, and it thus seems likely that the composer deliberately did not attach a slur.

Fantasia 6, d minor, TWV 40:7
- *1 49:4 This note appears doubled in the first edition. I have left the note ♪ due to the possibility that the composer may have forgotten to delete the note ♪. (See bar 52)
- *2 85:1 A crotchet in the first edition. Revised by the composer to a minim.
- *3 96:4 Revised by the composer from ♪ to ♪.

Fantasia 7, D major, TWV 40:8
- *1 1: See p. 46, 'The French Overture'.
- *2 7:1–2 & 8:1–2 The rhythm in the first edition is ♪♪♪♪ but it is performed with the rhythm ♪♪♪♪. See p. 47, 'The French Overture'.
- *3 78:6 Revised by the composer from ♪ to ♪.

Fantasia 8, e minor, TWV 40:9
- *1 14:5 The dynamic indication ƒ appears in the first edition, but I have deleted it in this edition because I have judged it to be an error on the part of the composer.
- *2 52:7 Revised by the composer from ♪ to ♪.
- *3 61:2 The first edition is somewhat unclear, but it would appear to be ♪. There are several editions that adopt this, but in this edition I have adopted ♪ due to the importance of the harmony (diminished seventh) at this point.

Fantasia 9, E major, TWV 40:10
- *1 9: The third beat is not present in the first edition. With reference to the fifth bar, I have assumed that the rest is missing.
- *2 47:6 Revised by the composer from ♪ to ♪.

Fantasia XI, G major, TWV 40:12
- *1 2:16 Revised by the composer from ♪ to ♪.
- *2 7:14 Revised by the composer from ♪ to ♪.
- *3 28: Perhaps due to lack of space, two beats are missing from the first edition. Various possibilities might be considered, but ♪♪♪ seems to be a valid performance possibility for the four beats.
- *4 42:4 The lack of clarity in the first edition means that it is difficult to say whether this should be ♪ or ♪. Since the harmonic progression from the first beat (dominant) to the second beat (tonic) at this point follows the same pattern as in bars 31, 35, 48 and 56, I have adopted ♪ in this edition so as to take account of the similar metrical sense in these bars. However, ♪ is also a possibility if one gives precedence to the sequential progression present in the bottom part with its descending third that appears from the sixth note in bar 41.

Fantasia XII, g minor, TWV 40:13
- *1 1:1 Revised by the composer from a crotchet to a minim.
- *2 67:5 Revised by the composer from ♪ to ♪.

各曲のスタイル / Stylistic features of each piece

有田正広 / Masahiro Arita

	ファンタジー Fantasie	全体 Overall	部 Parts	表示 Tempo and metre	様式・形式 Style and Form
即興へのアプローチ Improvisatory orientation	Fantasia 1 A major TWV 40:2	トッカータとフーガ Toccata and Fugue	1	Vivace: ¢	1〜10：プレリュード風トッカータ / Toccata à la Prélude 11〜26：フーガ / Fugue
				adagio –allegro	27〜36：アルペッジョと強弱のゼクエンツァの交代、そして第35小節からはフーガのテーマの断片がストロークで示され、次の部分へattaccaで導かれる / 27-36: Alternation between sequences of arpeggios and dynamics. A fragment of the fugue is marked with a stroke from bar 35, leading *attacca* into the next section
			2	Allegro: 3/8	メヌエット風 / In the style of a minuet
ソナタ形式へのアプローチ Sonata form orientation	Fantasia 2 a minor TWV 40:3	教会ソナタ Sonata da chiesa	1	Grave: 3/4	半終止で終わる序奏的な部分 / Introductory section ending on a half cadence
			2	Vivace: 3/4	
			3	Adagio: ¢	
			4	Allegro: 2/4	ブーレ風 / In the style of a bourrée
	Fantasia 3 b minor TWV 40:4	緩急が交代する部分とイタリア風ジグによる2部構成 2-part structure consisting of alternating fast and slow passages and an Italian-style gigue.	1	Largo –Vivace: ¢	単純な半終止を伴ったLargoがattaccaでVivaceへと導かれる Largo ending on a simple half-cadence leads *attacca* into the Vivace
			2	Allegro: 6/8	イタリア風ジグ Giga/Gigue in Italian style
	Fantasia 4 B flat major TWV 40:5	18世紀後半の（ドイツ地方の）ソナタ [緩–急–急] Sonata in late 18th-century German style [Slow, Fast, Fast]	1	Andante: ¢	18世紀後半（例えばベルリン楽派）のような緩徐楽章風 In the style of a slow movement from the late 18th century (e.g. Berlin school)
			2	Allegro: 3/4	
			3	Presto: ¢	ロンドーまたは三部形式 / Rondeau or three-part form
	Fantasia 5 C major TWV 40:6	3部分からなる自由な形式 Free form in three parts	1	Presto: ¢ – Largo: 3/2	句Traitのようなパッセージの短いトッカータ風とアリオーソ風のLargo Short toccata with Trait-like passages and Largo in arioso style
			2	Allegro: 9/8	フガートの要素を持った3小節フレーズの変奏曲風。ジグ風 Variations on a three-bar phrase with fugato elements. In the manner of a gigue
			3	Allegro: 6/8	カナリー風（シチリア風）/ In the manner of a canarie in Sicilian style
	Fantasia 6 d minor TWV 40:7	18世紀後半の（ドイツ地方の）ソナタ [緩–急–急] Late 18th-century sonata in German style [Slow, Fast, Fast]	1	Dolce: 3/4	18世紀後半にみられるような緩徐楽章風（たとえばベルリン楽派のような） Slow movement characteristic of the late 18th century (e.g. Berlin school)
			2	Allegro: ¢	単旋律楽器で表現する複雑な音の運びによって構成されたフーガ / Fugue consisting of complex melodic development presented on a monophonic instrument
			3	Spirituoso: 3/2	ロンド形式。6小節ごとにロンドーとクープレが交代する Rondo form. Alternation between rondeau and couplet every six bars
組曲へのアプローチ Suite orientation	Fantasia 7 D major TWV 40:8	フランス風序曲と民族舞曲的な要素の強いロンドー Overture in French style and rondo with pronounced folk dance elements	1	Alla Francese: ¢	1〜14：典型的フランス風序曲でグラーヴマン Gravement（＝荘重、壮麗）。次の3/8とはTempo relationで結ばれる / 1 to 14: Typical French-style overture with Gravement marking. Linked to following 3/8 section by tempo relation
			2	(Vite): 3/8 – ¢	15〜85：単旋律楽器で表現する複雑な音の運びのフーガ / 15 to 85: Fugue with complex melodic development presented on a monophonic instrument
			3	Presto: ¢	ロンド形式。8小節ごとにロンドーとクープレが交代する Ronde form. Alternation between rondeau and couplet every six bars
	Fantasia 8 e minor TWV 40:9	舞曲風な構成1 Dance-like structure 1	1	Largo: ¢	教会ソナタの緩徐楽章、あるいはアルマンド風（アルマンドによく見られる♪♪♪のリズムの使用）/ Slow movement in the style of church sonata. Use of ♪♪♪ rhythm as frequently evident in Allemandes
			2	Spirituoso: 12/8	イタリア風ジグ Giga/Gigue in Italian style
			3	Allegro: 3/4	3拍子に2拍子を感じさせ、奏者の遊び心を鼓舞する。ポーランド風舞曲とも捉えられる In a playful style in triple time but with suggestions of duple time. Intimation of a dance in Polish style
	Fantasia 9 E major TWV 40:10	舞曲風な構成2 Dance-like structure 2	1	Affettuoso: 3/4	フランス様式の低声部とイタリア様式の高声部が混合されたサラバンド Sarabande mixing French-style in lower part and Italian style in upper part
			2	Allegro: 3/8	
			3	Grave: 3/2	嬰ヘ音を基音とする属七和音から始まる即興的な音楽。この和音はホ長調のドッペル・ドミナントを担い、第83小節の属和音を経て第84小節の主和音に至る / Improvisational music beginning on the dominant seventh with F sharp as the tonic, functioning as the double dominant of E major. After passing through the dominant at bar 83, the tonic is reached at bar 84
			4	Vivace: 2/4	ブーレ風 / In the manner of a bourrée
	Fantasia X f sharp minor TWV 40:11	3つの舞曲 Three dances	1	A tempo giusto: 3/4	イタリア風コレンテ / Corrente in Italian style
			2	Presto: ¢	イタリア様式のガヴォット風 / In the manner of a gavotta in Italian style
			3	Moderato: 3/8	メヌエット（フランス風）/ Minuet in French style
ヴィルトゥオーソ演奏へのアプローチ Virtuosic orientation	Fantasia XI G major TWV 40:12	演奏技法への試み Virtuosic approach	1	Allegro: ¢	アルペッジョで始まるトッカータ風。第3部の終わりまでをひと続きに演奏する In the manner of a toccata beginning with arpeggios. Performed without a break up to the end of Part 3
			2	Adagio: ¢	第1部と第3部を繋ぐ即興的な部分 / Improvisational section linking Part 1 with Part 3
			3	Vivace: ¢	AllegroからVivaceまでをひと続きに演奏する / Performed without a break from the Allegro through to the Vivace
			4	Allegro: 6/4	舞曲風 / In dance style
	Fantasia XII g minor TWV 40:13	ファンタジーへの新しい試み New experimental approach to the Fantasy	1	Grave: 3/2 – Allegro: 3/4	Tempo relationをもとにした緩–急の交代。第62小節からは第19小節以降のモティーフの再現 / Alternation of slow and fast sections based on tempo relations. Reappearance of motifs from bar 19 onwards in the section beginning at bar 62
			2	Presto: ¢	ブーレ Bourée風。GraveからPrestoまで全曲を途切れなく演奏する / In bourrée style. Performed without a break from the Grave through to the Presto section

用語小辞典 〜18紀音楽を演奏するために
有田正広

Allemande(仏) アルマンド／Allemanda(伊) アッレマンダ →Fantasia 8
Allemandeとはフランス語で「ドイツの、ドイツ人の、ドイツ語の」を意味し、古くはパヴァーヌ PavaneやバスダンスBasse danceを源とすると考えられている。その名称から、沈着で思慮深く、荘重な雰囲気をたたえた音楽として17〜18世紀のフランスで流行した。曲想にはGravement(荘重な)、Moderement(控えめで節度のある)や、Gracieux, Gracieusement(厳かで優美、魅力的な)などの形容を用い、テンポはゆったりと遅い。殆どの場合♩♫／♪のアウフタクトを持ち、曲には16分音符が多く使われる。一方イタリアでは演奏に重点が置かれた軽快なAllegroまたはAllegro moderatoで、𝄵、4/4、時として2/4で記され、多くの場合は♪／♩のアウフタクトを持つ。

Arioso アリオーソ →Fantasia 5
ゆったりとしたアリア風な旋律で作られる楽章、または部分。18世紀にはレチタティーヴォRecitativo(叙唱)—Ariosoといったように、他の様式と対峙させた例が多く見られる。

Articulation アーティキュレーション
楽譜に記されることは現代に比べて限定的だったが、何も記されていない音符にも適切なアーティキュレーションが求められる。その中にあって、楽譜に記されているアーティキュレーションは、作曲者もしくは記譜者の強い音楽的要請によって書かれているものだと言える。何も記されていない音符のアーティキュレーションについては、以下のようなことが一般的には言えるが、**それはあくまで原則でしかなく、絶対的なものではない。**
◎ 順次音程：つなげる
◎ 跳躍音程：切る
◎ 三度音程などで和音を作るとき：
　　　　　　ある程度、適切に切る。ただしつなげる場合もある。
◎ 弱拍から強拍に向かうとき：拍感が壊れないように適宜に切る。
しかしこれ以外にも和声上の理由からスラーに近く演奏する場合もあり、アーティキュレーションの可能性が広い。各々の楽曲のテクスチュアを読み込むことで、バロック音楽の適正なアーティキュレーションを見出したい。

Bourrée ブーレ →Fantasia 2, 9, XII
フランスのオーヴェルニュ地方の民族舞曲で、単純な2拍子(2, 2/2, 𝄵)または4/4で記される。陽気で活き活きした速いテンポの弾むようなリズムで、多くの場合はアウフタクトを伴い、♪、♫や♩、時には♪が用いられる。

Canarie カナリー →Fantasia 5
スペイン、カナリア諸島のテンポの速い舞曲。2、6/4、6/8で書かれ、リズムは♩. ♪♩／♩. ♪／♫♫に必ず♪／♪／♫などのアウフタクトが付く。カナリーより少しだけテンポの速いイタリア風ジガ⇒Gigaと混同されやすい。

Courante(仏) クーラント／Corrente(伊) コレンテ →Fantasia X
フランス語で「流れる」を意味するcourirの過去分詞に由来する、なめらかな動作が特徴の舞曲。単に流れるだけではなく、自発的に「動く」「動き続ける」舞曲でもある(ラテン語には「走る」の意のcurrere、英語には「流れる、走る」の意を内包するcurrentの語がある)。ルネサンス期には3拍子のガリアルドGalliard／ガイヤールGaillardと結びついていたが、17世紀フランスでは高貴な宮廷人の舞曲へと変化した。多くの場合、拍子は3/2、3と書かれ、18世紀に入ると3/4の表記も出てくるが、フランス様式のクーラントは3拍子の中に変拍子を思わせるような拍感が特徴。イタリアでは演奏に重点が置かれることになり、フランス様式よりいくぶん軽快なテンポで、3/4の中に連続する単純な8分音符が目立ち、フランス様式とは一線を画す。

French Overture フランス風序曲 →Fantasia 7
ルイ14世統治下のフランスでリュリなどによって様式化されたオペラの序曲と、それを模した器楽作品。王の威厳の象徴である付点音符や勢いのある音階を特徴とする荘重、壮麗な堂々とした音楽。多くの場合2/2、𝄵、2と記され、4/4、𝄴で書かれることもある。Gravement、Fièrment、Lentementなどの表示を伴うゆったりとした2拍子を基本とし、記譜上の付点音符は、演奏上では複付点音符化する(たとえば♩♪は♩. ♬または♩..♬で、♩♪は♩. ♪で、♩... ♪は♩. ♪♬で演奏される)。また、音階も拍の後半に詰めて演奏する習慣が一般的だった。

3部形式をとり、中間部にはフーガまたフガート⇒Fugatoによるテンポの速い音楽が置かれ、最後に再び最初と同様に壮麗な音楽で曲が結ばれることが多い。しかし最後の部分は省略されることもある。緩−急−緩の3部分各々のテンポは、17〜18世紀の音楽に多く見られるテンポ・リレーション⇒Tempo relationに基づいて設定される。

Fugato フガート →Fantasia 1, 5, 6, 7
厳格な対位法的書法に基づいて楽曲全体を構成するフーガFugaの要素を取り入れた楽曲。

Gavotte(仏) ガヴォット／Gavotta(伊) ガヴォッタ →Fantasia X
16〜17世紀初期のガヴォットは男女のカップルで踊るブランルBranleと呼ばれる軽快な輪舞だった。17世紀後半になると2拍のアウフタクトを備え、第1、第2ガヴォットが対を成す例も出てくる。多くの場合、拍子は𝄵、2、2/2、2/4で書かれるが、時として4/4で記されることもある。イタリアではGavottaと綴られ2/4の表記が目立ち、演奏することに重点が置かれたものが多い。

Gigue(仏) ジグ／Giga(伊) ジガ／Jig(英) ジグ →Fantasia 3, (5), (8)
古くはイギリスやアイルランドの船乗りたちが船の看板で激しく活発なステップで踊った舞曲。イギリスではJigまたはJiggと綴り、「暴れる」の意を持つ。速いテンポの6/8、9/8、12/8拍子で♫♫♩ ♪などのリズムが連なる。

17世紀後半のフランスでは気品と格調をそなえたポリフォニックで複雑な書法で♪│♫♫.♫♫♫│♪.♫♫♫♫♫などのリズムが用いられるようになり、それに従ってテンポが遅くなった。イタリアでは元来の単純なリズムの♪│♫♫♫♫│♪│♪が用いられ、フランス様式に比べて速い。

J. S. バッハは16分音符を基本とした6/16、9/16、12/16の各拍子による特別なジグを書いており(たとえばフルートとオブリガート・チェンバロのためのソナタ ロ短調 BWV 1030、フランス組曲第5番 BWV 816、パルティータ第4番 BWV 828など)、これらはフランス、イタリアの様式とは異なる。バッハの弟子のキルンベルガーの記述によれば、バッハは8分音符と16分音符を分母とする拍子を混同することなく作曲しており、後者はあまりアクセントを付けずに急速な速度で演奏される。

Menuett(独) Minuetto(伊) Menuet(仏) メヌエット →Fantasia 1, X
時代とともに様々なステップが考案され、多種多様に変化していった最もポピュラーな舞曲の一つ。3/4、3/8、3と記され♩♩♩│♩♩♩のステップや、各4分音符ごとのステップなど、そのテンポの決定には音楽作品への洞察が必要。基本的にはAllegrettoの速度で、時として3/8のパスピエと混同されることがある。パスピエではヘミオラ♫♫♫♫♫♫が終止形に限らず他の場所でも用いられるが、メヌエットでは終止形の部分で用いられるのが常。

Prelude 前奏曲 →Fantasia 1
「〜の前に」「早期に」などの意味を持つ接頭語のPreと「奏する、動作する」などの語源を持つludere (ludus)から生まれた音楽用語がプレリュードPrelude。前奏曲、序奏として楽曲の一番最初に置かれる。バロック期においては①即興演奏(=譜面は残されないか、即興のメモ程度に残される。例えば17世紀にはフランスのPreludes non mesurés*など)と②即興的な要素をもとに作曲されたもの、または③前奏、序奏としての性格を有した楽章。

曲の内容や様式は様々だが、和声的な構造をもとにした句(トゥレ)⇒Traitの表現を用いて次に続く楽曲への期待感を醸成する。

*拍のない和声の流れが主体となったプレリュード。L. クープラン、ダングルベールなどのチェンバロ曲を参照のこと。

Rondeau ロンドー／Rondo ロンド →Fantasia 4, 6, (7)
平易な旋律で作られた1フレーズを主題として、別の旋律の挿入句と主題とを交代させることから成る楽曲。フランスでは主題をロンドー、挿入句をクープレCoupletと呼んでいる。

例　ロンドー ― 第1クープレ ― ロンドー ― 第2クープレ ― ロンドー ― 第3クープレ ― ロンドー　など。

Sarabande（仏）サラバンド／**Sarabanda**（伊）サラバンダ　　→Fantasia 9
サラバンドは15〜16世紀の南米またはスペイン、ポルトガルが起源とされる舞曲。肌を露わにした女性が淫らな姿で熱狂的に踊るところから、長い間宮廷には入れなかった。17世紀になり、作曲家たちが歌謡的要素を加えたり、単純な和声に変化をもたらすと、サラバンドは次第に宮廷の重要な舞踏曲へと変化した。拍子は3/4で記す。17世紀イタリアでは♩ ♩／♩. ♩／♩ ♩ ♩のバスの動きを基本とするゆったりとした歌謡性の高い音楽となったのに対し、フランスでは♩ ♩／♩ ♩. ♪などのバスの動きを基本として1拍目と2拍目に拍感を強めるなど、ドラマティックで深い情感を表現する書法を用いることが多かった。イタリアでは遅めのテンポを、フランスでは速めのテンポをとる傾向があるが、一概には言えない。

Trait トゥレ　　→Fantasia 5
短いセンテンスで作られた楽句で、多くの場合は素早い音楽で作られる。

Tempo relation テンポ・リレーション　　→Fantasia 7, XII
複数楽章間、あるいは同一楽章内でテンポが変化する際の、テンポ設定に関する基本的な概念。各々のテンポは比率関係から求められることが一般的だった。対峙する2種類の音楽の拍子感を共通のものとするこの考え方には定まった邦訳が無いが、「関連付けられたテンポ」とでも訳せる。後のリステッソ・テンポ L'istesso tempo（等しいテンポ）へとつながる。特にフランス風序曲⇒French overtureとそれに続くフーガまたはフガート⇒Fugatoではテンポ・リレーションの役割が重要になる。

例1：Fantasia 7, D major, TWV 40:8

◎2拍子的（当時の慣習に適ったもの）

◎4拍子的（理論上はあり得るもの）

例2：Fantasia XII, g minor, TWV 40:13

Toccata トッカータ　　→Fantasia 1, XI
「〜に触れる、さわる、動かす」の意を持つ動詞Toccareが名詞化したもので、楽器や音、音楽に触れた状態から生まれた楽曲のこと。曲想は⇒Preludeと似た発想だが、パッセージや音階、和声、アルペッジョを即興的にすばやく演奏することを目的としている。17世紀以降には、中間部にゆったりとした緩徐部分（⇒AriosoのようなAdagio部分）を配することがあった。

Glossary of musical terms
for performance of 18th century music

Masahiro Arita

Allemande　　→Fantasie 8
Allemande is the adjectival form of the word 'German' in French, and as a musical genre is thought to have its origins in the *Pavane* and *Basse dance* styles. The genre gained popularity during the 17th and 18th centuries as music with a contemplative and solemn atmosphere. Reflecting this mood, the tempo markings of the Allemande are customarily such as *Gravement, Modérément, Gracieux* and *Gracieusement*, all implying a slow and relaxed tempo. In most cases the music begins on an upbeat in forms such as (♪)♬♬ / ♬ / ♪ and makes extensive use of semiquavers. In contrast, in Italy, where emphasis tended to be placed on performance, the *Allemande* (*Allemanda* in Italian) was characterised by a fast tempo (Allegro or Allegro moderato) in ₵, 4/4 or sometimes 2/4, and generally beginning with an upbeat in the form of ♪ / ♩.

Arioso　　→Fantasie No. 5
A movement or section based on a slow aria-like melody. During the 18th century the term was frequently used in opposition to other formal categories, for examples in the manner of *Recitativo – Arioso*.

Articulation
Although articulation is less frequently indicated in early musical notation than it is today, appropriate articulation is obviously required even on notes on which no instructions for articulation appear. This implies that when articulation is indicated in the notation, it reflects a strong prescriptive intention of the composer or whoever has notated the music. The following general rules can be laid down in connection with the articulation of notes that bear no such instructions, but **they should not be regarded as applicable in all instances**.
   Stepwise intervals: Slurred
   Intervallic leaps: Detached
   Creating chords through the use of thirds, etc.:
      Detached to some extent, although sometimes slurred.
   From weak beats to strong beats:
      Ensure that the sense of metre is not lost.
But there may be other cases where, for harmonic reasons, slurs are required in performance, meaning that there is a wide variety of possibilities for articulation. Appropriate articulation of Baroque music requires a close reading of the texture of each piece.

Bourrée　　→Fantasias 2, 9 and 11
The *bourrée* was a folk dance originating in the Auvergne region of France and is notated in simple duple (2, 2/2, ₵) or quadruple (4/4) time. Bourrées are performed at a lively, fast tempo and in most cases begin on an upbeat with a prevalence of ♪, ♬, ♩ and sometimes ♪.

Canarie　　→Fantasia 5
The canarie was a fast dance piece originating in the Canary Islands. The rhythm is generally ♩. ♪ ♩. ♪ or ♩. ♬ ♬ with invariable use of upbeats in forms such as ♪♩, ♪ and ♬. The *canarie* is easily confused with the slightly quicker Italian-style gigue (*giga*).

Courante (It. Corrente)　　→Fantasia X
The word *courante* derives originally from the Latin word *currere*, meaning 'to run', as does the English word 'current' with its sense of 'flowing'. The *courante* is the name of a dance piece with smooth, flowing movements. During the Renaissance era it became linked with the three-beat *galliard* (or *gaillard*) and thus transformed into a noble court dance in 17th–century France. It is generally notated in 3/2 or 3 time, with 3/4 coming into use in the 18th century, although a feature of the *courante* in the French style is the sense of metrical irregularity present within the overall triple time structure. In Italy the *corrente* tended to emphasise instrumental virtuosity and would be performed at a slightly quicker tempo than that of the French-style *courante*. A feature in this case is the presence of a stream of simple quavers, thus setting the *corrente* apart from courante.

French overture　　→Fantasia 7
The French overture refers to overtures in the style perfected in France during the reign of Louis XIV by composers such as Lully and other instrumental works in this style. The genre is characterised by a mood of solemnity and grandeur generated through the use of dotted rhythms and dynamic scales that symbolised the magnificence of the royal court. Most overtures in this style are set in 2/2, ₵ or 2 time, although occasionally in 4/4 and ₵ time. They are often marked with slow-tempo expressive indications such as *Gravement, Fièrement* and *Lentement*, and the dotted notes are customarily performed in double

dotted fashion (e.g. ♩♪ as ♩..♪ or ♩.♪; ♩.♪ as ♩..♪; and ♩...♪ as ♩..♪♪). It was also common for fast scale passages to appear in the second half of a beat. French overtures were customarily in ternary form with the central section featuring fast music in fugal or fugato style, after which the piece would end with the reappearance of the same solemn music that appeared at the start, although the final section might sometimes be omitted. The tempi of the three fast-slow-fast sections was determined by the tempo relations frequently found in music of the 17th and 18th centuries.

Fugato →Fantasias 1, 5, 6 and 7
Fugato refers to pieces that incorporate fugal elements throughout the piece on the basis of strict contrapuntal writing.

Gavotte →Fantasia X
During the 16th and early 17th centuries the *gavotte* was a lively round dance performed by male and female couples deriving from the earlier genre known as the *branle*. During the latter half of the 17th century, the *gavotte* tended to consist of two contrasting pieces beginning with two upbeats. Set in duple metre, most *gavottes* employ the time signatures ₵, 2, 2/2 and 2/4, although 4/4 also occasionally appears. The Italian *gavotta* is generally set in 2/4 time and emphasises instrumental virtuosity.

Gigue →Fantasia 3, (5), (8)
The jig was originally a dance with lively steps performed by British and Irish sailors on board their ships. In Britain and Ireland the word was spelled either 'jig' or 'jigg', the latter term having bawdry connotations. Jigs are performed at a fast tempo in 6/8, 9/8 or 12/8 time.

In its late 17th–century incarnation in France, the *gigue* (from the English) came to employ rhythms such as ♪|♩.♫ ♫♫♫♫♫|♩ ♪|♩.♫ ♫♫♫♫♫ and to be based on sophisticated and tasteful polyphonic writing, with a consequence slowing of tempo. In Italy on the other hand the original simple rhythm ♪|♫♫ ♫♫|♩ ♪|♪ continued to be used in the *giga* with tempos faster than those employed in the French *gigue*.

J.S. Bach composed many *gigues* in a distinctive style based on semiquavers with the time signatures 6/16, 9/16 and 12/16, examples of which include the Sonata for flute and obbligato harpsichord in F minor, BWV 1030, the French Suite No. 5, BWV 816, and the Partita No. 4, BWV 828, all of which differ from the French *gigue* and the Italian *giga*. According to his pupil Johann Philipp Kirnberger, J.S. Bach composed without every confusing metre rooted in quavers and semiquavers, and in the case of semiquavers would perform them at a fast tempo without accentuation.

Minuet →Fantasia 1, X
The minuet was one of the most popular dance forms and changed in a variety of ways over the years with many new steps being constantly devised. The time signatures 3/4, 3/8 and 3 were generally employed, while the dance steps tended to change either every beat or every two beats ♩ ♩ ♩ | ♩ ♩ ♩ . Close consideration of the musical content is needed to determine the most appropriate tempo. As a rule the minuet is performed at an Allegretto tempo and is sometimes difficult to distinguish from the *passepied* in 3/8 time. In the *passepied* hemiolas ♫♫ ♫♫ | ♩ ♩ ♩ appear in various position rather than just at cadences, but in the case of the minuet they tend to be used solely at cadence points.

Prelude →Fantasia 1
As a musical term prelude refers to a piece that is played (Latin *ludere*) before (*pre-*) another piece and thus appears at the start of a work. During the Baroque era the term had three main meanings. First, it referred to an improvisatory performance given either with no notation whatsoever or on the basis of musical ideas jotted down by the performer. Preludes in this style include the *Préludes non mesurés* ('Preludes without fixed metre') popular in France during the 17th century, examples of which appear in the harpsichord music of Louis Couperin and Jean-Henri d'Anglebert.

Rondo →Fantasias 4, 6, (7)
The rondo was a musical form that takes as its theme a single phrase made up of a simple melody which then alternates with other melodic interpolations. In France the theme was referred to as the *rondeau*, while the interpolations were known as couplets.

Example: Rondeau – 1st couplet – Rondeau – 2nd couplet – Rondeau – 3rd couplet – Rondeau, etc.

Sarabande →Fantasia 9
The *sarabande* was a dance originating in Latin America, Spain and Portugal during the 15th and 16th centuries. Originally a frenetic dance in which women's exposed their bare bodies, the *zarabanda* was banned in Spain on account of its obscenity and was not permitted entry into European courts. At the start of the 17th century the *sarabande* underwent a transformation as a consequence of composers adding song elements and simple harmonies, thus gradually changing into a dance form that occupied an important position in the court. *Sarabandes* employ the 3/4 time signature. In Italy during the 17th century the *sarabande* (*sarabanda* in Italian) turned into a genre with a highly song-like character in a slow tempo with a bass line in the form of ♩ ♩/♩. or ♩ ♩ ♩, while in France it was common to employ a dramatic and deeply emotional expressive language that involved strengthening the accents on the first and second beats and with a bass line in the form of ♩ ♩ or ♩ ♩.♪. The tempo of such pieces tended to be slow in Italy but faster in France, although generalisations concerning tempo should be avoided.

Trait →Fantasia 5
A *trait* is a passage consisting of short sentences generally performed at a fast tempo.

Tempo relations →Fantasia 7, XII
When changing the tempo between separate movements or within the same movement itself, it was customary to determine the tempo on the basis of proportional relations. This was especially the case in genres such as the French overture and the ensuing fugal or fugato sections.

Example 1: Fantasia 7, D major, TWV 40:8

– Duple metre (according to contemporary custom)

– Quadruple metre (theoretically conceivable)

Example 2: Fantasia XII, g minor, TWV 40:13

Toccata →Fantasia 1, XI
Toccata is the nominal form of the Italian verb *toccare*, meaning 'to touch'. The musical term appears to have come into existence in the sense of 'touching' or 'coming into contact' with an instrument, sound or music. The music is similar in character to that of the prelude, but the main aim of the genre was to allow for fast improvisational performance of passagework, scales, harmonies and arpeggios. From the 17th century onwards a slow section in the form of an adagio in the arioso manner would sometimes be placed in the middle.

(Translation: Robin Thompson)

参考文献 Bibliography

Burton, Anthony, ed. *A Performers Guide to the Music of the Baroque Period*. ABRSM, 2001. アントニー・バートン編, 角倉一朗訳『バロック音楽 歴史的背景と演奏習慣』音楽之友社, 2011.

Grebe, Karl. *Georg Philipp Telemann: In Selbstzeugnissen Und Bilddokumenten*. Rowohlt, 1970. カール・グレーベ著, 服部幸三・牧マリ子訳『テレマン—生涯と作品』音楽之友社, 1981.

Sachs, Curt. *Eine Weltgeschichte Des Tanzes*. D. Reimer/E. Vohsen, 1933. クルト・ザックス著, 小倉重夫訳『世界舞踊史』音楽之友社, 1972.

浜中康子著『栄華のバロック・ダンス 舞踏譜に舞曲のルーツを求めて』音楽之友社, 2001

Quantz, Johann Joachim. *Versuch Einer Anweisung Die Flöte Traversiere Zu Spielen*. Johann Friedrich Voß, 1752. ヨハン・ヨアヒム・クヴァンツ著, 荒川恒子訳『フルート奏法 [改訂版]』全音楽譜出版社, 2017

Kirnberger, Johann Philipp. *Die Kunst des reinen Satzes in der Musik*. G. J. Decker und G. L. Hartung, 1774. ヨハン・フィリップ・キルンベルガー著, 東川清一訳『純正作曲の技法』春秋社, 2007年

Paulsmeier, Karin. *Notationskunde 17. Und 18. Jahrhundert*. Schwabe, 2012. パウルスマイアー著, 久保田慶一訳『記譜法の歴史 モンテヴェルディからベートーヴェンへ』春秋社, 2015

Die Musik in Geschichte Und Gegenwart. 1st ed., "Telemann" by Martin Ruhnke, Bärenreiter, Metzler, 1966

Petzoldt, Richard. *Georg Philipp Telemann*. Translated by Fitzpatrick Horace. Ernett Benn Limited, 1974.

Gottfried, Walther Johann. *Musikalisches Lexikon Oder Musikalische Bibliothek* 1732. Edited by Richard Schaal. Facsimile ed. Documente Musicologica. Kassel: Barenreiter, 1953

The New Grove Dictionary of Music and Musicians: Vol 18, Oxford University Press., 1995.

Brossard, Sébastien. *Dictionnaire de musique*, Christophe Ballard, 1703.

Rousseau, Jean–Jacques. *Dictionnaire de musique*, Veuve Duchesne, 1768

Le Blanc, Hubert. *Defense de la basse de viole*, Pierre Mortier, 1740

Mattheson, Johann, *Grundlage einer Ehren Pforte*, Johann Mattheson, 1740

Mattheson, Johann, *Das neu-eröffnete Orchestre*. Johann Mattheson, 1713

Isherwood, Robert M. *Music in the Service of the King: France in the Seventeenth Century*. Cornell University Press, 1973.

Powell, Ardal. *The Flute*. Yale University Press, 2002.

Hotteterre Le Romain, Jacques. *Principles of the Flute: Recorder & Oboe*. Translated by David Lasocki. Barrie & Rockliff: the Cresset Press, 1968.

Ruhnke, Martin. *Georg Philipp Telemann, Thematisch–systematisches Verzeichnis Seiner Werke: Telemann–Werkverzeichnis* (TWV). Bärenreiter, 1984.

Telemann, Georg Philipp. *Musique De Table* 1733. Edited by Barthold Kuijken. Facsimile ed. Franz Biersack. 2010.

Telemann, Georg Philipp. *Der getreue Music–Meister* 1728. Edited by Michel Giboureau. Facsimile ed. 2004.

Telemann, Georg Philipp. *12 Fantasias for Flute solo*. Edited by Barthold Kuijken. Musica RARA 1987.

Telemann, Georg Philipp. *12 Fantasien für Flöte solo*. Edited by Peter Reidemeister. Amadeus BP370. 1992.

Telemann, Georg Philipp. *Sonate Metodiche*. 1728/1732. Facsimile ed. S. P. E. S.

有田正広

桐朋学園大学、ブリュッセル王立音楽院、デン・ハーグ王立音楽院を卒業。NHK・毎日音楽コンクール（現・日本音楽コンクール）ブルージュ国際音楽コンクールのフラウト・トラヴェルソ部門で第1位を獲得。ルネサンスから現代に至る400年間に変遷を遂げたさまざまなフルートを駆使する演奏は、さまざまな時代の作品に輝かしい光を与え、人々を魅了しつづけるアーティストとして高い評価を得ている。アルヒーフ、DENONアリアーレ、avex-CLASSICSから録音リリース多数。第21回サントリー音楽賞受賞。現在、昭和音楽大学教授、桐朋学園大学特任教授。2018年第30回 ミュージック・ペンクラブ音楽賞クラシック部門特別賞を受賞。全10巻のDVDシリーズ「有田正広 公開講座 17〜18世紀の音楽演奏法について 音楽の裏に潜む情感を訊ねて」（村松楽器販売株式会社）が発売されている。

Masahiro ARITA

He is known all over the world for playing the flute in its many different incarnations as used throughout music history. With his tireless study and matchless musicality, he entrances audiences by brilliantly illuminating the works of various eras. He graduated Toho Gakuen School of Music, Royal Conservatory of Brussels, and Royal Conservatory of Music in the Hague, and won First Prize at the Mainichi Music Competition and in the flauto traverso category at the Bruges International Music Competition.

His work as a flautist within Japan is also quite distinguished, and he takes Part in many recitals, ambitious concerts, programs, and chamber series. Arita is best known for his mastery of many different incarnations of the flute, as it has changed over the course of the 400 years since the Renaissance. His recordings, are released on Archiv, Denon Ariale, and avex-CLASSICS. In 1989 he received the 21st Suntory Music Award. He is a Professor at Showa university of Music, Distinguished Professor at Toho Gakuen School of Music.

テレマン 無伴奏フルートのための12のファンタジー TWV 40:2-13 [原典版]

2018年7月10日 第1刷発行
2024年6月30日 第7刷発行

校訂　有田正広
発行者　時枝正
発行所　株式会社 音楽之友社
東京都新宿区神楽坂6の30
電話 03(3235)2111(代)　〒162-8716
振替 00170-4-196250
https://www.ongakunotomo.co.jp/

609043

© 2018 by ONGAKU NO TOMO SHA CORP., Tokyo, Japan.

落丁本・乱丁本はお取替いたします。
Printed in Japan.

本書の全部または一部のコピー、スキャン、デジタル化等の無断複製は著作権法上での例外を除き禁じられています。また、購入者以外の代行業者等、第三者による本書のスキャンやデジタル化は、たとえ個人や家庭内での利用であっても著作権法上認められておりません。

楽譜浄書：加賀屋浄書
翻訳：ロビン・トンプソン
装丁：吉原順一
印刷／製本 (株) 平河工業社